Prophet Muhammad ﷺ Receives the First Revelation

Shazia Nazlee

Goodwordkidz

In the days before Islam, many of the Arab people did not know how to read or write. For those who could, it was a better gift than anyone else had, for it was only the rich who had all the best things in life.

It was Islam that brought knowledge to people, whether rich or poor.

ISL

The command to "read" was the first word to be revealed to the Prophet Muhammad ﷺ by the Angel Jib'rail.

At the age of 40, whilst married to Khadijah, the Prophet Muhammad ﷺ would often spend a lot of his time deep in thought. He would think about the way the world works , the people in it, etc.

One of his favorite places
for meditation was the
Cave of Hira, on Mount
Nur, which was very close
to Makkah.

One day, whilst the Prophet was in the cave, all of a sudden, the Angel Jib'rail appeared in front of him and said: "Read!" But the Prophet replied: "I cannot read."

So the Angel caught hold of the Prophet, hugged him very tightly until it hurt. He then let go and said to the Prophet: "Read!" Once again the Prophet replied: "I cannot read."

Again the Angel hugged him tightly till the Prophet ached. Then he let go and said: "Read! In the Name of your Lord who created. He created man from a clot. Read! Your Lord is the Most Generous. He has taught by the pen. He has taught man what he did not know."

These were the very first verses of the Quran revealed to the Prophet Muhammad ﷺ. The *surah* to which these verses belong is known as *surah al-Alaq*. It reminds us about the creation.

Read!

In the Name of your Lord who created. He created man from a clot.

Read!

Your Lord is the Most Generous. He has taught by the pen. He has taught man what he did not know.

بِسْمِ اللهِ الرَّحْمٰنِ الرَّحِيمِ

اِقْرَأْ بِٱسْمِ رَبِّكَ ٱلَّذِي خَلَقَ ۞

خَلَقَ ٱلْإِنْسَانَ مِنْ عَلَقٍ ۞

اِقْرَأْ وَرَبُّكَ ٱلْأَكْرَمُ ۞

ٱلَّذِي عَلَّمَ بِٱلْقَلَمِ ۞

عَلَّمَ ٱلْإِنْسَانَ مَا لَمْ يَعْلَمْ ۞

15

The Prophet at this point was very scared. He left the cave and went straight home to his wife Khadijah. He said to Khadijah: "Cover me", as he was trembling with fear. He explained to her what had happened in the cave.

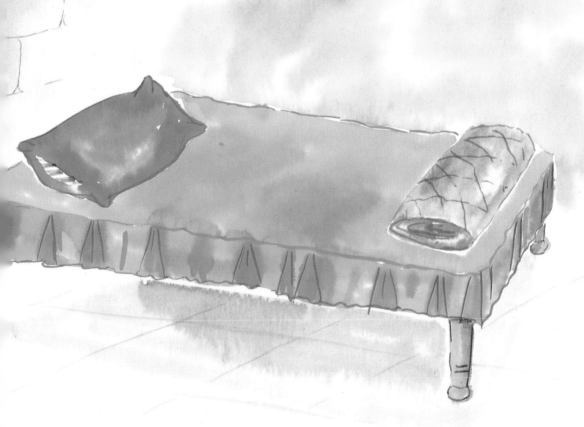

This is the story of how the very first verses were revealed.

The first eight verses remind every human being about Allah's favors to us: how He created us and how He bestowed upon us all this knowledge.

The rest of this *surah* refers to the Prophet's uncle, Abu Jahl. Abu Jahl would always try his very best to stop the Prophet Muhammad ﷺ from praying in the Ka'bah.

Once when the Prophet was praying
at the Ka'bah, Abu Jahl came up to
him and said: "Did I not forbid you to
pray here? If I see you praying here
again, I will punish you."

We, as believers, should always remember Allah's favors to us, such as the knowledge, which He has given us to help us to worship Him. We should show Allah our gratitude by worshipping Him and obeying His every command.

Answer the questions below by ticking (a) or (b).

1. The Prophet Muhammad's favourite place for sitting and thinking deeply was:

   a) the Cave of Hira;   b) the Ka'bah.

2. Which Angel came to see the Prophet?

   a) Izra'il;   b) Jibra'il.

3. What was the first word the Angel said to the Prophet?

   a) read;   b) speak.

4. The Prophet, who was very frightened, went straight to his wife:

   a) Khadijah;   b) Aishah.

5. The Prophet then went to visit Waraqah who told him to be:

   a) careful;   b) silly.

6. Who does the rest of the Surah describe?

   a) Abu Lahab;   b) Abu Jahl.